For katie from Talia

UNPLUG WITH SCIENCE BUDDIES

BODY ODDITY PROJECTS

Floating Arms, Balancing Challenges, and More

Rebecca Felix

Lerner Publications ◆ Minneapolis

Lerner Publications Company

A division of Lerner Publishing Group, Inc.

241 First Avenue North

Minneapolis, MN 55401 USA

For reading levels and more information, look up this title at www.lernerbooks.com.

Main body text set in Zemestro Std Book 12/16

Typeface provided by Monotype Imaging Inc.

Photo Acknowledgements

The images in this book are used with the permission of: Design elements and doodles © Artur Balytskyi/Shutterstock Images, © Mighty Media, Inc., © owatta/Shutterstock, © primiaou/Shutterstock, © Sashatigar/Shutterstock, © STILLFX/Shutterstock, © Tiwat K/Shutterstock, © Tom and Kwikki/Shutterstock, © vesves/Shutterstock, and © yoyoyai/Shutterstock; © Radachynskyi/iStockphoto, p. 4 (colored blocks); © Imgorthand/iStockphoto, p. 5; © Anastasiia Boriagina/iStockphoto, p. 6; © Mighty Media, Inc., pp. 7 (scissors, ruler, notebook, pom-poms, pens), 8–29 (project photos); © siur/iStockphoto, p. 17; © LightFieldStudios/iStockphoto, p. 30

Front and back covers: © Mighty Media, Inc.

Library of Congress Cataloging-in-Publication Data

Names: Felix, Rebecca, 1984– author.

Title: Body oddity projects : floating arms, balancing challenges, and more / Rebecca Felix.

Description: Minneapolis : Lerner Publications, [2019] | Series: Unplug with science buddies | Audience: Ages 7–11. | Audience: Grades 4 to 6. | Includes bibliographical references and index.

Identifiers: LCCN 2018058306 (print) | LCCN 2019003096 (ebook) | ISBN 9781541562431 (eb pdf) | ISBN 9781541554948 (lb : alk. paper) | ISBN 9781541574885 (pb : alk. paper)

Subjects: LCSH: Human body—Experiments—Juvenile literature. | Human physiology—Experiments—Juvenile literature. | Biology projects—Juvenile literature. | Science—Experiments—Juvenile literature.

Classification: LCC QP37 (ebook) | LCC QP37 .F45 2019 (print) | DDC 612—dc23

LC record available at https://lccn.loc.gov/2018058306

Manufactured in the United States of America

Contents

Your Body Unplugged

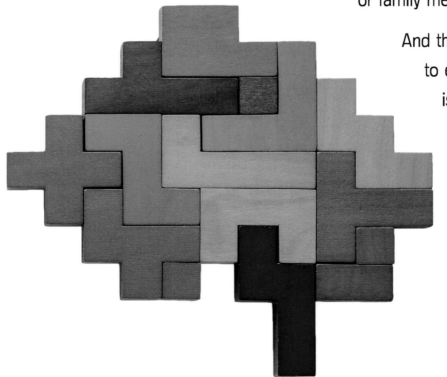

Have you ever wondered how your body balances as you stand, sit, and bend over? Or the science behind how we see color?

You can learn a lot about science by exploring the functions of your body. And you don't need fancy lab equipment, computer software, or other technology to do it! All you need is your body, a few household items, and, for some activities, friends or family members.

And the fun doesn't need to end once the activity is over. Think of ways to experiment more or gather more data. What can you discover? Let's unplug and start making!

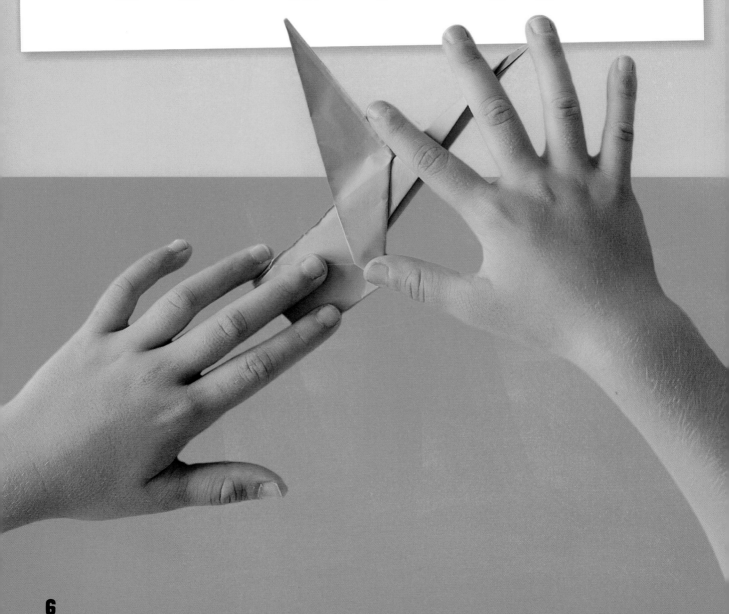

Before You Get Started

SUPPLY CHECK

Many of the projects in this book use common household items and craft supplies. These can include paper, markers, and scissors. Other materials can be found at the grocery store, hardware store, or office supply store.

SAFETY FIRST

The projects in this book involve body movements. When completing an activity, take care not to get hurt. Ask an adult for help when needed.

CLEANING UP

When you've completed an activity, remember to clean up! Put supplies and furniture back where you found them and clean up your workspace.

SEEING AFTERIMAGES

Discover how staring can temporarily change the way our eyes see color!

MATERIALS

- ☆ 3 sheets of white paper
- ☆ small, round lid
- ☆ pencil
- ☆ markers (red, green, and blue)
- ☆ stopwatch or timer

SCIENCE TAKEAWAY

We have three types of cone cells in our eyes. Each type responds to a different color: red, green, or blue. When all cone cells are triggered at the same time, we see the color white. Staring at one color tires out the cone cells that respond to that color. Then, when you look at a sheet of white paper, all cone cells are triggered, but the tired ones don't respond. So, the two other types work together. For example, without the response of the red cone cells, you see white as a blend of green and blue!

1 Trace the lid three times along a long edge of a white sheet of paper.

2 Color the three circles red, blue, and green.

3 Cover the blue and green circles with the other sheets of paper.

4 Stare at the center of the red circle for 30 seconds. Then, look at the white space next to the circle. What do you see?

5 Cover the red and green circles with the other sheets of paper.

6 Stare at the center of the blue circle for 30 seconds. Then, look at the white space next to the circle. What do you see?

7 Cover the red and blue circles with the other sheets of paper.

8 Stare at the center of the green circle for 30 seconds. Then, look at the white space next to the circle. What do you see?

FOOT SENSING

Use only your hands to identify objects. Then, find out if your feet can achieve the same feat!

MATERIALS

☆ 20 familiar objects:

   Each object should be at least the size of your fist or as long as your finger.

   Can include toys, foods, household objects, and clothing.

   Make sure none of the objects are breakable or have sharp edges.

☆ volunteer
☆ sticky notes
☆ markers
☆ chair
☆ blindfold (a scarf works well)
☆ stopwatch or timer

SCIENCE TAKEAWAY

Receptors in our skin help us sense an object's shape, texture, and size. A person can often identify something just by touching it with their hands. This is harder using feet for two reasons. First, our hands are more flexible and have longer digits than our feet, which makes touching and holding objects easier. Second, our hands have been trained from a young age to do these tasks.

1 Place the objects where your volunteer can't see them.

2 Write "wrong" on two sticky notes. Draw a hand on one and a foot on the other.

3 Repeat step 2 but write "right" on the notes.

4 Place the hand notes on the floor on one side of the chair. Place the foot notes on the floor on the other side of the chair.

5 Have your volunteer take off their shoes and sit in the chair. Make sure your volunteer's feet reach the floor. Blindfold your volunteer.

Foot Sensing continued on next page

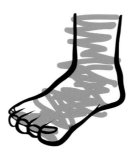

6 Place an object in your volunteer's hands. Give them 10 seconds to guess what it is.

7 If your volunteer's guess was incorrect, silently place the object near the "wrong" hand note. If the guess was correct, set the object near the "right" hand note.

8 Repeat steps 6 and 7 with nine more objects.

9 Repeat steps 6 and 7 with the remaining ten objects. But this time, have your volunteer use their feet to feel the objects! Place the objects near the "right" or "wrong" foot notes after each guess.

10 Remove your volunteer's blindfold. Review the piles together. Did your volunteer guess correctly more often using their hands or their feet? Can you think of a reason why?

INTERFERENCE OPTICAL ILLUSIONS

Optical illusions use color, light, and patterns to fool our brains into seeing things that aren't there. Create this tricky type of imagery with everyday objects!

MATERIALS

☆ 2 identical pocket combs
☆ colored construction paper
☆ 2 identical metal or nylon meshes, such as window screens

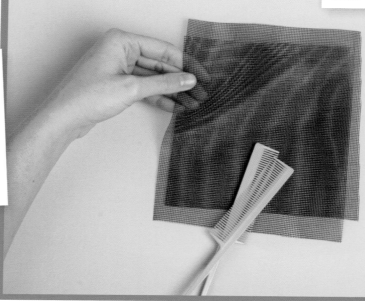

SCIENCE TAKEAWAY

When two objects with identical patterns overlap, but their patterns do not line up exactly, new patterns become visible. These are moiré patterns. They are optical illusions! Moiré patterns only occur in objects with patterned holes or spaces. Moving the objects changes the spaces between their identical patterns. This interferes with, or blocks, some light, creating the illusion.

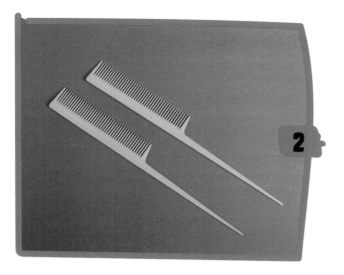

COMB ILLUSION

1 Choose a sheet of construction paper that is a very different color from the combs.

2 Place the combs next to each other on the paper. Examine their tines. How would you describe them? Are they far apart or close together? Do they make a repeating pattern?

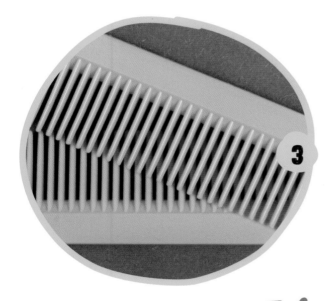

3 Place one comb on top of the other. Move the top comb slightly. Observe the overlapping tines. Do they create a new pattern?

4 Continue moving the top comb up and down and side to side. Then, rotate the combs. What do you see?

Interference Optical Illusions continued on next page

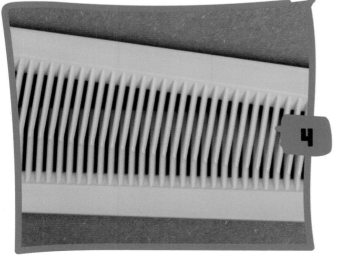

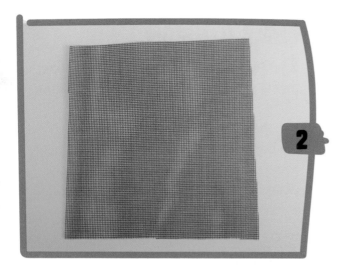

SCREEN ILLUSION

1 Choose a sheet of construction paper that is a very different color from the screens.

2 Place one screen on the paper. Examine the screen's square patterns.

3 Place the second screen on top of the first. Are new patterns created?

4 Move the top screen slightly up and down and side to side. Try lifting its corners or edges to bend the material. What do you see?

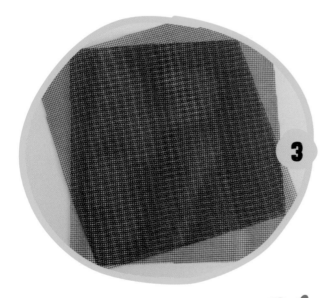

FLOATING ARMS

Can you cause your body to create an involuntary movement in your arms? This is a type of movement your brain doesn't plan to happen!

MATERIAL
☆ open doorway

SCIENCE TAKEAWAY

Sometimes your body moves your muscles without you thinking about it. These are involuntary movements. Your brain tells your arm muscles to press against the doorframe. When you step away, your muscles are still pushing up, making your arms lift. This involuntary movement happens until you think about stopping it. Then your brain blocks the muscles' lift signal and you can lower your arms.

1 Stand inside the doorway. Raise both arms until the backs of your hands touch the doorframe. Press your arms against the doorframe while slowly counting to 60.

2 Step out of the doorway and relax your arms. What happens?

3 If nothing happened to your arms, repeat steps 1 and 2. But this time press your arms harder against the doorframe.

4 Repeat the activity, but press your arms into the doorframe for a count of 30. Do the results change?

5 Repeat the activity pressing just one arm into the doorframe. Or, try rotating your hands to press against doorframe with your palms. What happens?

BRAIN NAME GAME

Our brains sometimes associate certain shapes with sounds. Use two silly, made-up words to test this!

MATERIALS

☆ marker
☆ 12 index cards
☆ paper
☆ 3 or more volunteers

SCIENCE TAKEAWAY

The brain makes connections between shapes and sounds. People tend to label round shapes "bouba" and sharp ones "kiki". Some scientists believe this happens because B is a softer-sounding letter than K. When you say "bouba" your mouth makes a rounded shape, which better matches the rounded drawn shapes.

1 Draw a pointy, star-like shape on six index cards. Make sure the shapes are all a little different.

2 Draw a round, cloud-like shape on the other six cards. Make sure the shapes are all a little different.

3 Draw two columns on a sheet of paper. Label one "expected." Label the other "unexpected."

4 Shuffle the cards together.

5 Tell your volunteer that you are going to show them twelve pictures. For each one, the volunteer should say if the drawing is "bouba" or "kiki." If your volunteer asks what these words mean, tell them you cannot explain. Your volunteer simply has to make their best guess.

6 Have your volunteer name each shape one at a time. Make a tally in the "expected" column each time the volunteer identifies a round shape "bouba" and a pointy one "kiki." Make a tally in the "unexpected" column for each opposite guess.

7 Repeat steps 4 through 6 with at least two more volunteers.

8 Review your data. Which column has the most tallies? Why do you think this is?

SEE AND SPEAK: COLOR TRICK

Can the brain name the color it sees instead of the word it reads? Test your friends and family to find out!

MATERIALS

☆ 15 index cards
☆ scissors
☆ markers (5 colors)
☆ stopwatch or timer
☆ paper
☆ pencil
☆ 3 or more volunteers

SCIENCE TAKEAWAY

When most people look at a word, their brains automatically read it. When a card's ink color matches the word, it is easy for volunteers to say the color of the ink. This is because it matches the word their brain reads. When the ink color is different from the word, the task is harder and takes more time!

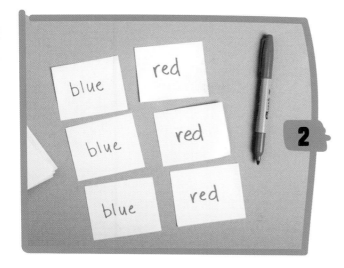

1 Cut the index cards in half to create thirty smaller cards.

2 Use each marker to write its color on three cards.

3 Use each marker to write different colors on three cards. For example, use the blue marker to write "red," "green," and "brown."

4 Keep the cards from step 2 separate from those in step 3. Shuffle both stacks of cards.

5 Place the cards from step 2 facedown in front of a volunteer. Tell the volunteer to flip each one over and say out loud the color of the ink as quickly as they can. Time how long it takes them to get through the stack. Record the time.

6 Repeat step 5 with the cards from step 3.

7 Repeat steps 4 through 6 with more volunteers. Review the times you recorded. Which stack of cards took the volunteers longer to get through? Why do you think this is?

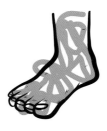

ARM LIE DETECTOR TEST

Turn a friend or family member into a living lie detector to explore the connection between the brain, body, and lying!

MATERIALS

- ☆ volunteer
- ☆ paper
- ☆ pen or pencil
- ☆ stable stool or chair (only needed if your volunteer is much taller or shorter than you)

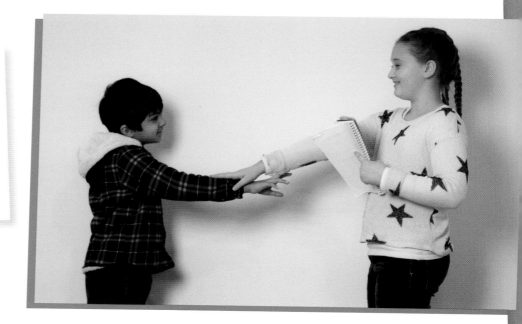

SCIENCE TAKEAWAY

The brain works harder when we lie and when we do two tasks at once. This is why it is easier to push down your volunteer's arm when they are lying. Their brain has to focus more on the lie and so has less focus on resisting your push. When your volunteer tells the truth, their brain doesn't have to focus so hard on what they are saying. So, they can focus more on resisting your push.

1 Ask your volunteer to complete the following sentences three times each. They should choose something different but truthful for each one. Write down the six sentences.

> I strongly dislike ____.
>
> I really like ____.

2 Stand facing your volunteer. Each of you should raise one arm straight in front of yourself, palms facing down. Move so your hand is right above your volunteer's hand. If necessary, the shorter person should use a chair or stool until your arms are at about the same level.

3 Tell your volunteer you are going to have them say some sentences and that you will push down on their hand as they say them. They are to try and keep their arm up.

4 Rest your palm on top of the volunteer's hand and wrist. Read a sentence from step 1 aloud. Ask the volunteer to repeat it. Push down steadily on their arm as they speak. Repeat for all six sentences.

5 Repeat step 4, but this time, replace the liked and disliked things with things you make up. Try to choose things that would be untrue to your volunteer! For example, "I really like vomit" would be untrue for most people. Was it easier or more difficult to push the volunteer's arm down when they were speaking the truth or lying?

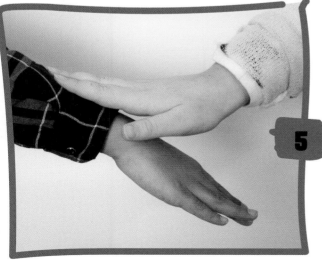

BALANCING CHALLENGES

Can you defy gravity and complete these fun balance tests?

MATERIALS

☆ wall to lean against
☆ volunteer
☆ small object
☆ ruler

SCIENCE TAKEAWAY

Your body has a center of mass. Gravity pulls on it. When standing up, your center of mass is above your feet, so you feel balanced. Leaning right moves your center of mass to the right. Leaning forward shifts it forward. Away from a wall, you can shift your body to stay balanced when your center of mass moves. When leaning against a wall, you cannot shift. So, you feel too unbalanced to lift your foot or bend over!

CHALLENGE ONE

1 Stand several feet away from the wall with your feet together. Keep your back straight and your arms at your sides.

2 Try to lift your left foot behind you without moving your right foot. You can bend your knees, but you must keep your arms at your sides. Are you able to hold your foot up without falling over?

3 Lean the right side of your body against the wall. Make sure your right foot, right hip, and right shoulder are touching the wall.

4 Repeat step 2. Now are you able to lift your left foot more easily? Why do you think this is?

Balancing Challenges continued on next page

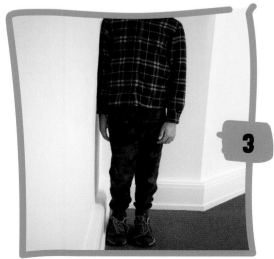

CHALLENGE TWO

1 Stand with your back against the wall. Place your feet together, with your heels touching the wall.

2 Ask your volunteer to place the small object on the floor about 1 foot (30 cm) in front of you.

3 Try to bend over at the waist to pick up the object. Do not bend your knees or move your feet! Are you able to pick up the object?

4 Take a step away from the wall. Place your feet together. Ask your volunteer to place the small object on the floor about 1 foot (30 cm) in front of you.

5 Try to bend over at the waist to pick up the object. Do not bend your knees or move your feet! Now are you able to pick up the object? Why do you think this is?

Explore More!

What fun or odd body activities did you try? What did you learn about your body? Science is all around us, even when we aren't plugged into technology. And the more we experiment with science, the more we discover. So keep exploring new ways to discover the science behind the human body!

FURTHER INFORMATION

For more information and projects, visit Science Buddies at https://www.sciencebuddies.org/.

Farndon, John. *Stickmen's Guide to Your Awesome Body.* Minneapolis: Hungry Tomato, 2018.

Olson, Elsie. *Memory Fun: Facts, Trivia, and Quizzes.* Minneapolis: Lerner Publications, 2018.

Rhatigan, Joe. *Wacky Things about the Human Body: Weird & Amazing Facts about Our Human Bodies!* Lake Forest, CA: Walter Foster Jr., 2019.

Glossary

achieve: to do something successfully after trying

associate: to form a connection between things in your mind

automatically: done without thinking about it

blindfold: a scarf or other material that is tied around the head to cover the eyes and block the wearer's vision

cell: one of the tiny parts that make up all living things

center of mass: the point in an object or structure where an equal amount of mass is on each side

digit: a finger or toe

flexible: able to bend

gravity: the force by which all objects in the universe are attracted to one another

identical: exactly the same

illusion: something that looks or seems different from what it is

involuntary: not done willingly or by choice

receptor: an organ or cell able to respond to light, heat, or other stimuli and send a signal to the nervous system

texture: the way something feels when you touch it

tine: one of the thin, pointed parts of a fork or comb

Index